A Fun Day With Nana

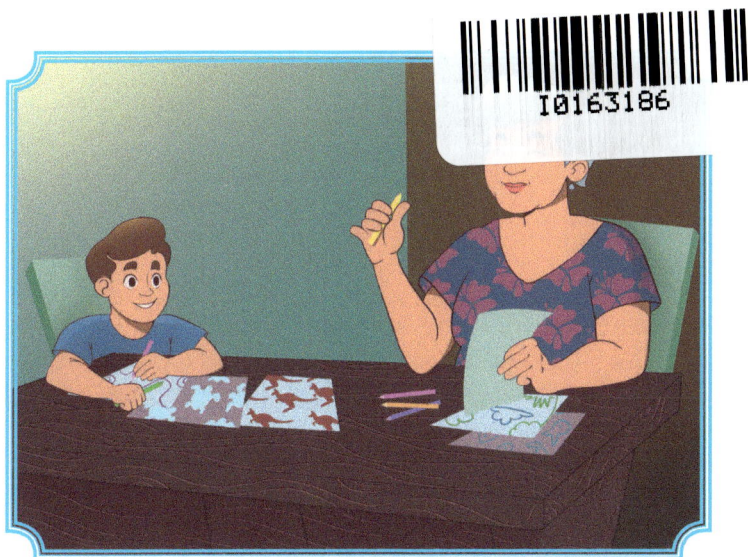

By Sonia Sharpe

Library For All Ltd.

Library For All is an Australian not for profit organisation with a mission to make knowledge accessible to all via an innovative digital library solution. Visit us at libraryforall.org

A Fun Day With Nana

First published 2023

Published by Library For All Ltd
Email: info@libraryforall.org
URL: libraryforall.org

Our Yarning logo design by Jason Lee, Bidjipidji Art

Original illustrations by Paulo Azevedo Pazciencia

A Fun Day With Nana
Sharpe, Sonia
ISBN: 978-1-922991-95-9
SKU03386

A Fun Day With Nana

Eoghan and Nana had
a day out.

We dropped my brother at
school then drove about.

First, we went to the museum and looked around.

We even went to the part where there was light and sound.

Next, we went to lunch
and had a feed.

Nana bought a book so
we could read!

Then we went to the park
to have a play.

But a thunderstorm came,
and so we ran away.

At last, we went inside
to do some drawings.

A day with Nanna is
never boring!

You can use these questions to talk about this book with your family, friends and teachers.

What did you learn from this book?

Describe this book in one word. Funny? Scary? Colourful? Interesting?

How did this book make you feel when you finished reading it?

What was your favourite part of this book?

download our reader app
getlibraryforall.org

About the author

Sonia was born in Newcastle on Awabakal Land and loves spending time with her family. She adores being around her precious grandchildren — seeing their perspective on the world they live in keeps her young. As a child she loved *Tin Tin* and *Asterix*.

Darwin

NORTHERN
TERRITORY

QUEENSLAND

WESTERN
AUSTRALIA

SOUTH
AUSTRALIA

Brisbane

NEW SOUTH
WALES

Perth

Adelaide

Sydney

ACT
Canberra

Author's Country

VICTORIA
Melbourne

TASMANIA
Hobart

Our Yarning

Want to discover more books from this collection? Our Yarning is a collection of books written by Aboriginal and Torres Strait Islander peoples across Australia.

We know that children learn better, and enjoy reading more, when they see themselves in the stories, characters and illustrations of the books they read.

To download the app, visit the Google Play Store on any Android device and search 'Our Yarning'.

www.ingramcontent.com/pod-product-compliance
Lightning Source LLC
Chambersburg PA
CBHW042345040426
42448CB00019B/3416